If You Tell Me,
I Can Fly!

Sharon Thayer

Illustrated by Linda Nagy

Believe and you will fly!

Sharon Thayer
2014

If You Tell Me, I Can Fly!

Written by Sharon Thayer
Illustrated by Linda Nagy
Scientific consulting by Tristan Kubik
Edited by Sharon Roe · Sharon@SharonRoe.com
Graphic design by Hancey Design · www.HanceyDesign.com

Inquires should be sent to:
Carousel Publishing, Inc.
info@Carousel-Publishing.com
www.Carousel-Publishing.com

Cataloging-in-Publication Data
Thayer, Sharon
If You Tell Me, I Can Fly!
            p. cm.
1. Inspiration 2. Success 3. Young adult
I.Sharon Thayer II. If You Tell Me, I Can Fly!
ISBN 978-0-9766239-1-5 Hdk
LCCN: 2014902158

Printed in the United States
By Worzalla Publishing Company
www.worzalla.com

This book is dedicated to those who
see the strengths, visions, and dreams of others
and take time to give instruction, encouragement,
and sometimes a little push
for the pure joy of watching them fly!

Thank You!

A special thank you to
Marlene Everson Roberts
for seeing my vision and for the push!

A caterpillar
inched along,

listening to a message:

a soft echo inside.

"I can fly!" she dreamed,
   as she sunned her chrysalis,
      and soon emerged a butterfly.

And she flew!

First exploring,

a baby hummingbird spied a hovering neighbor,

with such speed of beating wings.

"You can fly!

What looks impossible is just not so.

Believe, and you can fly."

And he flew!

Only hours old,

a little bumblebee looked from his nest,

as the queen bee whispered,

"You can fly!

 With your heavy body and dainty wings,

  don't ask why—just fly!"

And he flew!

Upon a leaf,

a ladybug larva dreamed out loud,

"How I wish I could fly."

"You will soon fly.

Keep your dream alive and give it time,"

said a friend passing by.

And she flew!

An eaglet hops

back and forth across his nest.

His father calls as he soars by,

"Put your wings to the test.

You can fly!

Take your first leap!

I believe in you, now fly!"

And he flew!

A young girl emerges

from childhood's cocoon,

with dreams inside as big as the sky.

Alone at future's edge,

she glances back to her teachers, family, and friends.

"If you tell me, I can fly…"

And she flew!

Author
Sharon Thayer

When the last of my three children moved away from home in 2001, I started writing. At that time I had no idea how many stories were to come. The faster I wrote, the faster the ideas came flowing out. After writing for over ten years, I began to publish. My stories are grouped into three series of books: Holiday Tales, Inspirational Fables, and Memorial Memories. Each story is woven together with messages of ethics, values, and self-esteem, and is targeted to touch your heart on the brink of greatness, in the toast of celebration, or the embrace of sorrow.

The first book in the Inspirational Fables series, *If You Tell Me, I Can Fly!*, was born one day as I thought how much easier it would be to reach my goals if someone simply said, "You can do it!" We all crave those powerful words that can make a tremendous difference in our lives.

As I wondered how many people stand on the edge of their dreams and never take the next step, I thought, what if someone told them, "I believe in you"? What if someone told them they could fly? What if I told them? So I wrote a story to tell people everywhere of every age, "Follow your dreams. You can succeed. You can fly!"

My first book in the Holiday Tales series, *The Myth of Santa's Beard,* was honored in 2013 with a bronze metal from both the Moonbeam Children's Book Awards for Holiday Books and the Colorado Independent Publishers Association for Children's Picture Books.

Upcoming books include:
> Inspirational Fables: *The Biggest Dream, Catch Me Moon,* and *The Hole Story*
> Holiday Tales: *A Tooth Fairy Named Mort, Cupid's Reminder,*
> *When the Easter Bunny Gets the Flu, Dancing on the Rainbow* (St. Patrick's Day), and
> *What the Scarecrow Knows* (Halloween).
> Memorial Memories: *God Gave Her Wings, God Gave Him Wings,*
> *The Path We Walked Together* (In memory of your dog), and
> *Waiting at the Gate* (In memory of your cat).

Illustrator
Linda Nagy

Born in Atlanta, Georgia, Linda has been fascinated with art since childhood. She attended the University of Georgia where she earned BFA and MFA degrees in graphic design. Her career began at Hallmark Cards in Kansas City, Missouri, where she designed greeting cards in watercolor media.

Returning to Georgia, she worked for several years as a layout artist before establishing a retail and direct marketing business with her husband, Bernie. In their off time they traveled extensively throughout the United States, Europe, South America, and New Zealand, as Linda's eclectic style constantly evolved, reflecting new techniques and influences. The rich tapestry of events in Linda's life has influenced her art, but color is the dominant feature which permeates all her work.

Now retired in South Park, Colorado, Linda and Bernie write and publish Colorado nature books. Their successes include two award-winning coffee table photo books; *Colorado's South Park: High Country Paradise*, with three first place Colorado Independent Publishers' EVVY awards and two International Book Awards in 2010, and *South Park, Colorado: Nature's Paradise* claiming three first place CIPA EVVY Awards plus the prestigious Past President's Award. Their latest project published in 2014 is *Rocky Mountain Wildflowers Field Guide*.

Linda's artwork may be seen at www.HighCountryArtworks.com.

Scientific Animal Facts

The animals in this book were chosen because of their unique way of becoming creatures of flight.
Below are facts about how each comes to fly.
I wish you luck in discovering your own unique way to 'fly'!
– Sharon Thayer

Hummingbird:
Mature hummingbirds beat their wings 12-80 times per second while their hearts beat 12 times per second.* To sustain this behavior, they require a nectar-rich diet in addition to a healthy number of insects.

Butterfly:
When a caterpillar sheds its skin, it becomes a chrysalis. Within the chrysalis, the original body converts into a protein soup, and not even the brain or heart survive this transformation. Slowly the soup is rearranged into a butterfly, which then breaks its way out of the chrysalis. After pumping blood into its wings, it flies.

Bumblebee:
Most insects that have rapid wing flight, like the bumblebee, move their wings in a rotation pattern. This pattern works with the wind. A conventional flap, like that of a bird, works against the wind. This rapid wing flight motion saves a lot of energy for the insect and allows heavier weight to be lifted per wing surface area.

Ladybug Beetle:
Ladybug beetle larvae survive only if they can avoid ant threats and feast on aphids. This aphid feast occurs for several weeks, and then the larva pupates. As a pupa, the prior larva grows wings and the ability to fly, and therefore can escape from the ants as an adult ladybug beetle.

Eagle:
Eaglets are fed vigorously for the first month or so in preparation for their fledgling flight. The eaglets can practice flapping their wings by hopping from branch to branch or across the nest, but the first departure from the nest is the final test. Either they fly or fall to their death.

*Hummingbird statistics supplied courtesy of Wikipedia.org.

Carousel PUBLISHING

Carousel Publishing's mission is to produce products with quality of life messages for children of all ages. The programs outlined below are some of the ways we assure our products get into the hands and hearts of children.

Donation Program: Many times the children who most need a special story or an inspirational message are not in a place where they can receive such a gift. Carousel Publishing partners with individuals and corporations in gifting books to nonprofit organizations serving children. In the past, we have helped to gift our books to children at Ronald McDonald Houses, shelters, hospitals, and schools. Please share your goals with us and we will do our best to help you succeed.

Fundraising Program: Carousel Publishing products are available at wholesale prices for fundraising projects. We do not require you to be a nonprofit organization to qualify for this program. Fundraising also may be combined with an Author Program.

Author Programs: Reading, signing, and educational programs can be designed with or without a fundraising component. With a minimum purchase guarantee, each person in attendance will receive a copy of an illustration from the book, signed by the author. Please contact us about our current programs.

Contact Carousel Publishing at Sharon@carousel-publishing.com to reserve your date!